DUST STORMS MAY EXIST

poems

Praise for *Dust Storms May Exist*:

What a map toward hope Ben Groner offers in *Dust Storms May Exist*. Drifting between travelogue, confession, elegy, and ode, these poems scour mythic American landscapes for anything enduring and true. Here live muttering quail, mosquitoes torqued as pumpjacks, patchy alfalfa, fog scarfing fir trees—even grime on a concrete overpass is held, witnessed, sung into record. Groner, the seeker, hands us vignettes where the cosmic meets the commonplace, where loss and discovery converge into one message, a single destination in this enormous world full of souls: advance.

—Allison Adair, author of *The Clearing*

Ben Groner III writes the kind of poetry that makes you stop and stare—at its beauty, yes, but also at the small, incandescent details to which it calls your attention. In *Dust Storms May Exist*, a paper-clip burn becomes a meditation on friendship, bodily ailments open space for contemplating landscapes and travel, and the simple gesture of stepping aside on a canyon trail morphs into a conversation about life's endless inventories of chance. This is a stunner of a book, one that created the quietest of spaces where I could immerse myself in Ben Groner's many sojourns across exquisite terrains made even more so by his unwavering curiosity, his keen ear, and his reverent wonder. I'm grateful for poems and poets like this. I'm grateful for the reminder to slow down, to take notice, and as the final words of the book suggest, to step into my own life.

—Destiny O. Birdsong, author of *Negotiations* and *Nobody's Magic*

Dust Storms May Exist is a stunning collection "drenched in gladness" and gorgeous imagery, striking that delicate balance between beauty and ache at the seam of each poem. Ben Groner III is a poet who pierces each moment with reverence and brilliant examinations of the human spirit searching through pastoral landscapes and histories for deep empathy and connection. A sense of awe travels throughout these poems as the speaker travels around the world "stunned into silence and stillness." These are poems abounding with faith, family, masterful closures, and exquisite lines like "A night heron rises from the river like a memory / about to return...." This book continually held my attention and my heart.

—Tiana Clark, author of *I Can't Talk About the Trees Without the Blood*

Ben Groner III's first collection of poems takes readers across the country and offers them a vision of an America worth embracing. In places like Hopkinsville, KY, Northern Mississippi, New Mexico, New Orleans, Toledo, Tucson, and beyond to the coastlines, we find people engaged in luminous daily life with homegrown geniuses like Faulkner and Lead Belly as backdrop and soundtrack. *Dust Storms May Exist* is a powerful book of odes and elegies, reflections on a father gone too soon and a country seemingly unraveling, like the "Untied States" on a sign remembered from a road trip. These are poems of travel and exploration, weathering storms of many kinds along the journey, always delivering a sense of rich and meaningful arrival.

—Jesse Graves, author of *Merciful Days* and *Tennessee Landscape with Blighted Pine*

Ben Groner III's whirlwind debut, *Dust Storms May Exist*, transports the speaker and reader across cities, countries, histories, and relationships—these are travel poems, if by "travel" one can mean insistent looking and revelation. However, it's not what the speaker sees that unites the collection—rather, it's the way he looks beneath and before and after what is in front of him to more fully see himself. Here is a speaker who can enter a foreign space and reach for the other to say, "I'm just as lost / inchoate, feeble, bewildered as you. / Just as thrumming, as resplendent." This is a book for anyone who wishes to do more than glance in foreign cities, anyone who has been in the C Boarding Group. Wherever you are going, take this book with you, and pick up where Groner leaves off.

—Lily Greenberg, author of *In the Shape of a Woman*

Ben Groner's poems often begin in observation, and often the place seems new to the poet as well as his readers. With wry humor and lyric patience, Groner invites us into the acutely alert and sensitive space of a true traveler, one whose canny, generous eye and ear lead us into revelatory explorations, not only of place, but of the true conditions of his life, those close to him, and our lives as well.

—Jeff Gundy, author of *Wind Farm*

Vastness in all its forms—sky, land, time, ache, faith, even language itself—is at the heart of Ben Groner's first collection, *Dust Storms May Exist*. From Bolivia to Chile, from Cana to Capernaum—and with so much "shimmering and shifting / around us"—Groner asks, "Where can one ground oneself?" Maybe there's no comforting, enveloping answer but, instead, only this radiant life where strangers—all sons and daughters—sometimes find themselves in shared spaces, marveling, attuned to the same mysteries where "so much can happen" and where "the dead are always with us." "One language can't tell the whole story," Groner says; and whether that story is personal or communal, local or global, momentary or eternal, perhaps all we can do is to trust "that what we see is being / held together, invisibly." Fortunately for us, Groner's poems reveal at least a glimpse of the shimmering, precarious, ecstatic proof.

—Jeff Hardin, author of *A Clearing Space in the Middle of Being*

With unrelenting awe, Ben Groner keeps "an eye to a viewfinder," patiently waiting, sure that revelation will come in the form of the "solitary hawk wheeling in the ephemeral dusk" or "particles of the sinking sun sifting / warmly through kitchen windows." Drawing from his childhood in Mississippi, the depths of loss, and the liberating landscapes of the American West and South America, Groner's flickering poems are elegies for every fleeting moment, recording what has changed and what endures "beyond the scar, the heat, the flame, / the momentary spark."

—Elizabeth Hughey, author of *White Bull*

In the engagingly varied poems of *Dust Storms May Exist*, Ben Groner III invites himself to remember, invites us to revel with him in the moments, the landscapes, the surprises in a life closely observed. "I'm not asking for revelation," he asserts. "I don't need to be taken anywhere." Paradoxically, his poems take us on a wide-ranging journey—from the concrete overpass and vacant railyard that open "Inventory of Pit Stops" to the street art of Valparaíso, Chile. Groner has an eye for the revelatory in small things. "For now," he says, "I want to live in that instant just before the sun / peeks out from behind the moon, and again floods the day with light." Open this collection to any page. Share in Ben Groner's wonder.

—David Meischen, author of *Anyone's Son*

In Ben Groner III's debut poetry collection, he asks, "Have you discovered a hidden key that unlocks joy?" Yes, an absolute yes, these poems, which are an amalgamation of landscapes, people, and sensory insights, is that key, a key that unlocked a curiosity within me. Groner is an expert in the interrogative, leaving readers with questions that linger on the tongue like, "Can one distinguish between yearning and loneliness / and love, or do they each taste the same," and "Harm or harmony—toward which will religion swerve?" Throughout the collection, Groner guides us through an inventory of pit stops that unearth revelations, ruminations, and superb scenes of the South. Open up this book, this key, this poetic map by Ben Groner III, and see what unlocks within yourself.

—Joshua Nguyen, author of *Come Clean*

DUST STORMS MAY EXIST

poems

BEN GRONER III

MADVILLE
PUBLISHING
Lake Dallas, Texas

FIRST EDITION

Requests for permission to reprint or reuse material from this work
should be sent to:

Permissions
Madville Publishing
PO Box 358
Lake Dallas, TX 75065

Cover Art: *Butte* by Grant Haffner
Cover Design: Jacqueline Davis
Author Photo: Emily April Allen

ISBN: 978-1-956440-85-0 paper; 978-1-956440-86-7 ebook
Library of Congress Control Number: 2023950526

Table of Contents

Following a circle would give a purpose—to come around again—where taking a straight line would not ... But how to begin a beginning?

—William Least-Heat Moon, *Blue Highways*

It is a strange thing, after all, to be able to return to a moment, when it can hardly be said to have any reality at all, even in its passing. A moment is such a slight thing, I mean, that its abiding is a most gracious reprieve.

—Marilynne Robinson, *Gilead*

I

THE WINDOW

In this rented room in this port city
far from home, I look up from the desk
out the window to where the violet sky
has been black for hours, the moon's
orb orange and enormous, the hills
wrapping around the bay draped
with a glittering net of streetlights.
There is a sense my entire life is out
there, verging and pulsing, waiting.
Maybe existence in any meaningful
sense requires both embodiment
and action. I bring my gaze back
into this little room, past the pale
blue window trim to the lime green
walls, tiny wooden dresser and closet,
slender mirror, cold empty bed.
I set my pen aside, close my journal,
turn out the light, the hills blazing and
shimmering in silence. I wonder how
long I have been holding my breath.

II

UNTIED

It was the first day of the road trip, and halfway between
our nation's capital and the site of the 1927 Bristol Sessions
we pulled off the highway, passing an abandoned sanitarium
which loomed above the town like a scab on the flesh of the land.

A few minutes later, we found ourselves on the dusty paths
of the Frontier Culture Museum, ambling backward through
time among traditional dwellings from England, Ireland, Germany
deconstructed and reconstructed on this land. A West African
compound of clay buildings and domed thatched huts crouched

off to the side. The architecture of American houses from
the 1740s, 1820s, and 1850s sang of how cultures intertwined,
how everything stems from something else—Irish women grew
squashes, okra, black-eyed peas. As we walked, we speculated

on the loneliness of the first man to hike from Pennsylvania
to this soil through an unforgiving winter, surviving without
shelter until he threw together a tiny primitive cabin of logs
sandwiched between thick layers of red mud, with disheveled
and flared boards for a roof that didn't help much against the rain.

Chuckling, we passed a sign that read "Untied States" while
espousing the merits of spelling books in early grade schools.
Even now, with this country stitched together by train tracks,
bridges, interstates, generations, trauma, societal norms—

there's still a risk of unraveling, of neighborly conversations
fraying around the edges. We found the 1850s house inhabited by
an elderly museum worker in a blue dress and white bonnet,
and as I studied its spacious whitewashed interior and brushed
an antique German *scheitholt* on a desk that would morph into

the mountain dulcimer, I heard my friend asking the sweet lady a string of questions. Upon striding out to the porch, she was explaining how as the West opened up in the 1800s, settlers sloughed off their native nationalities and started wearing

the word "American." Can a single word mean everything and nothing? We smiled goodbyes and set off across the lawn, but something compelled me to look back. The old woman was leaning against the doorway, waving and wishing us well on our journey. For a moment I felt as if I were her restless son leaving the homestead in search of a country I'd hardly seen.

Passing the schoolhouse, that adjective scrawled across my mind—*untied, untied*—then there was only the clear brightness of the September afternoon, the wind rippling the woman's blue dress and white bonnet, her hand waving us on and on and on.

FEED & SEED

Perhaps not one of us can go home
again, but who would want to?

A scarf of rainclouds wrapped around
the mountains as we drove to the quiet

town, where, not much later, we jogged
to the two-story brick building

on the corner of the quaint main street,
aiming for the dark green-and-cream

striped awnings shielding the door
from the glistening droplets as the last

light drained from the sky. The long
time-weathered sign, barely legible,

read "Fletcher Supply Co." and was
bookended by vintage Coca-Cola discs

the size of table tops. An historic plaque
mentioned these bricks were stacked

in 1919, the same year my grandfather
awoke to the world—the difference

being this building was still standing.
Inside, elderly couples shuffled

to bluegrass music: the fiddle piercing,
the banjo frenetic, the mandolin

like swollen drops of rainwater
pattering on shale. I couldn't escape

the sensation—who would want to?—
of her hands in mine as she taught me

to freestyle clog. I didn't know my heel
from a horseradish, but we stomped

on those creaky floors till sweat
soaked through our shirts, someone

whistling when I spun her. When we
paused for breath, an older man,

hunched and mustached, leaned over
and said, "Bluegrass on Fridays and

and Saturdays, church on Sundays!"
Well, that explained the pews, and how

places don't seem to have meaning
until people bestow it. At times,

we may need to pray; at others, we
need to dance. What are our bodies

supposed to do with space, with
themselves? We whirled the night

away until the band closed out their
set with Hank's classic gospel hymn.

Standing by the front pew, the whole
room singing, *I'll fly away oh glory*,

we let our shoulders lean and touch,
my eyes pressed shut, my lungs belting

out the tune with all their might,
feeling as if some unsayable place

within me had already taken flight.

TOTAL ECLIPSE

Hopkinsville, Kentucky, August 2017

We strangers—the Vietnam War vet, the graying woman,
    the pale teenager, and myself—stand near a telescope
in a high school parking lot to watch the moon open its mouth

and swallow the sun. Hard to believe it will happen, the morning
    so green-bright and heavy with heat. Roy, the veteran,
regales us with stories of visiting every U.S. Navy vessel

in the sea in 1975 while the woman smiles silently and I tinker
    with my camera's tripod. After so much waiting, does
readiness wax or wane? The celestial coins begin to rub together,

merging gradually, the light slowly silvering until it happens:
    a few seconds of shadows shimmying along the ground
like veins of sunshine underwater, then the sudden enveloping

dimness of standing in an enormous room when someone flips
    off the light switch. Stars blink on like streetlamps
warming up. A cold breeze riffles the sweetgum trees.

Somewhere nearby, a cricket rasps groggily. Everything feels
    surreal, the colors muted and all wrong, and above us
that black void, a perfect circle, like a tunnel to another galaxy,

an escape we didn't know we wanted, or needed. A diaphanous
    ring shimmers around the edge, and the woman
exclaims: "Isn't this thrilling?" as if we were all missing it,

and maybe we were. I fumble with my camera, trying in vain
    to snap a picture, then glance over and see the teenager
standing frozen, his mouth mirroring the eclipse, and I too am

stunned into silence and stillness. After all, how many hundreds
       of hours have we spent sitting in traffic, standing in line,
washing the dishes, brushing our teeth? I can't say, but for

these three minutes, we four strangers get to crane our necks
       toward a phenomenon so far beyond us, so blindingly near.
There's a sense it's been orchestrated (size, distance, perspective)

for our wonder, even as the laws of physics propel the objects
       farther along their orbits. In thirty seconds, we'll mumble
goodbyes, jump back into our trajectories and head back down

highways to cities and towns with their duties, sirens, walls.
       And though I already feel the moment slipping away
the way everything does—seawater through fingers, coins through

pocket holes—for now I want only enough time to behold
       the mystery above me, to live in that instant just before the sun
peeks out from behind the moon, and again floods the day with light.

NORTHERN MISSISSIPPI

Brother, do you remember? All those years ago? How sticky pinecones crunched and crackled when we stole into the silent woods, the moon above like a coin of butter melting into the frosty, misty midnight air, how our frozen fingers clutched flashlights as we followed the grownups with their rifles, you dashed ahead but I wasn't far behind, the heat of adventure pulsing hard in our chests, how we scoured the bony treetops and then: the telltale glint and crack of a shot, the coonhound's echoing howling haunting that dew-dusted meadow we pelted across, how blood welled from our hands and cheeks as we plunged into thorny brambles, and the carcass lay stiff by the maple's trunk as we stood, our breath kindling warmth, immortal—how it took all our strength to lift it by the tail, its death reeking of copper and shit, moonshine sloshing among the men, sips even burning our lips as the pine trees bowed to forgive us our silence.

A RECOLLECTION OF RAIN

a tintinnabulation of rain
on the tin roof

or—

I was underwater in the warm sheets,
the crackling of rain above me like last
night's fire, resin sizzling off the fat
pine, and was someone playing a piano?

here it is, I promise:

a December drizzle awakened me
gently, like a mother's touch, from
childhood dreams into an envelope
of electric blanket warmth, and through
silvery rivulets on the bedside window's
thick glass I glimpsed an early covey
of quail muttering, disappearing,
into the foggy Mississippi morning
wrapping grayly around skeleton trees
above deep jade gardens, the brick
courtyard a dried blood red, the world
singing an ode, or a lament, or both—

so, then,

a tintinnabulation of rain
on the tin roof.

BRIEF ILLUMINATION

There's a story my uncle once told me about a special train
that clattered past Parchman Penitentiary after midnight,

those headlights shining on the walls like Rosie's salvific breasts,
her outstretched hand holding official papers that would free

the sorriest of men. Lead Belly did time in cells such as those,
though not too much, seeing as how the governor of Texas liked

his strong, gravelly voice, how he made his 12-string Stella guitar
swell with low, rhythmic finger picking. An hour east of that rail line,

Peggy leans closer to me and whispers, "That is the prettiest thing
I ever heared" as my friend fiddles freely on the darkly lacquered

porch of my family's vacation home. This is the same Peggy who
served me pancakes and bacon as a boy, who will make sure we're

fed tonight, who will clean our sheets in the morning. Tomorrow,
my friend and I will kneel in the syrupy dusk among tufts of cotton,

those earthbound clouds that provide no shade. Her hands will finger
a boll, her eyes will glance over at mine as if to say: *You don't see this?*

My uncle said Lead Belly was a bad man, but he was pardoned.
This isn't such a bad land, but it's hushed, hardened. As night falls

I think of the mournful wail of that train whose fleeting light hit
every burgh on its way north, of the screeching hope on those rails.

Tomorrow, we'll inhale a last sweet breath of clay and pine, fire up
the engine, swerve around a desiccated armadillo, rattle on south.

THE BURN

The scar on my inner right forearm,
that inch of wrinkled skin that never
quite settled back into the color
it was born with—in it I see
my brother's face and our friend's
that night in his father's office
where we scorched a paperclip
with the lighter he stole
and pressed it to each of our arms,
as if friendship were something
you could seal in folds of flesh.
But do you really think I'm
talking about a stupid burn?
I haven't spoken to that friend
in over a decade, heard he left
college after slugging someone
in a drunken haze. I don't think
his burn lasted. I know my brother's
didn't. But as mine peers wordlessly
up at me now, I sense no regret,
only wisps of curiosity and sadness,
wondering what, if anything, lasts
beyond the scar, the heat, the flame,
the momentary spark.

THIRTY-THREE FOOTBALL FIELDS

So much can happen in a city, in a day,
especially when it's untethered and jubilant
New Orleans, and it's an afternoon in 1925.

Faulkner and Spratling have just finished
fabricating history and gossip while posing
as guides for a walking tour and are now

back in their apartment, shooting passerby
with BB guns through the wrought-iron
balcony—extra points for nuns—laughing

as they stir up juniper gin in the bathtub.
So much can happen in a street, in an hour,
Katrina's wailing vortex moved off

elsewhere, dissipating, as the macabre
sight of coffins floating down Canal Blvd
silences the saxophones, a reminder

the dead are always with us. The museum
placard says coastal wetlands are vanishing
at a rate of thirty-three football fields a day:

a hundred yards of land lost for every year
of Christ's life, or Crane's, nearly, lost at sea
until the day is yesterday or tomorrow or

a distant decade obscured from view by
the stone-gray clouds. So much can happen
in a swamp, in a second. An alligator

languishes, a mosquito scribbles
in the humid air, a mottled bald cypress
watches as the other trees quiver.

AT THE EDGE OF THE FOREST

Fall Landscape *by Julian Onderdonk, oil on board, 9in. x 12in.*

In the first days of October,
the clearing always looks the same—
a tangled sea of frenzied grass
keeping the bones of the birches
with their ocher crowns at bay,
the colossal tree my grandfather
showed me as a boy
set apart from the others, holy,
seeming to know more about
storms and droughts and seasons
than the rest of the woods,
its branches twisting and sprawling
"like our histories," he said,
clothed in plumes
of chestnut and fire and wine.

The breath of autumn is passing
as he did; softly, swiftly,
only the sound of a branch
breaking, a hip cracking,
taking with it the knowledge
the tree is just another scaffolding,
a sweat-beaded promise, a protest
against decay, a hope born
of pattern and chance and time spent
straining toward the sun, a desire
blossoming from a hundred years
of memory and anticipation as it bears
the weight of a robin's-egg blue sky
caught between summer and
winter, morning and night.

FOOTFALLS, A DECONSTRUCTED PANTOUM

There was a time
my father and I shared
the same air.

I'd been new to this
world, with so many days ahead,
but now

his smile is static in the silver
picture frame, his face weary
yet youthful
in the afternoon glow.

This world was news to me,
many days lay ahead
for me,

while his breaths were numbered
inside his chest, his tired face
youthful yet
in the evening gloam,

his presence closer than
my skin, my bones.

Though his breaths were
numbered inside his chest,
he used to jog, numb,

along wind-battered Ocean Drive.
His presence closer
than my bones, my skin,

I wonder if my footfalls
ever fit perfectly into his.

Once he jogged along the wind-shattered
ocean, but now
his smile is static
in the silver picture frame.

I wonder if
my footfalls ever fit perfectly
into his—

there was a time
my father and I
shared the same air.

CORPUS CHRISTI, OR AN EXPLORATION OF TIME AND SPACE

People say time travel
isn't real, but just yesterday

I passed through a salty
mesquite heat shimmer

into my childhood
bedroom, the very place

where I idled and grew
and imagined futures

in the filtering sunlight,
where my grandfather

kissed his wife goodnight
for the ten thousandth time,

where my father crawled,
marrow-thin and shattered,

into a coma, where—in
a nameless increment of

time—he exhaled his last,
rattling, baptismal breath.

MOSQUITOES

Four calves frolic
beyond the fence:
a tethered freedom.
Beneath their hooves
a mottled flint
arrowhead sleeps
in the caliche: a silent,
earlier life. The view
veers to mosquitoes:
pumpjacks plunging
into parched land.

RIVER RAIN

The canyon walls, the river,
all those trees that had been engulfed
in sun took on a new hue,
something more green, more blue.

A couple of hawks wheeled lazily
in the bright, domed backdrop like lovers,
a single cloud splayed across
the sky like a heavy, blanched galaxy.

From that gray, droplets fell
perforating the river's shell,
birthing bubbles kaleidoscopic
on the water's surface.

I knew the rain would merely
last a moment. What doesn't?
But its brevity made it gleam
all the more. Its want of eternity
spoke of forever.

IF MY PHYSICAL AILMENTS TOOK A ROAD TRIP

The alfalfa along Black Pine Road
is getting patchy, as are my eyebrows,
idiopathic ulerythema ophryogenes
uprooting those minuscule stalks
from sunburnt land. While we're at it,
let's not forget to properly position
the lumbar cushion for that most sinuous
of coastline curves, scoliosis that always
has my back. White lines stutter
on the blacktop, but it will relieve you
to know my right eye hasn't wandered
since childhood surgery, though I've
retained the tendency to meander down
blue highways, open to a rustic barn,
a timorous pond. Epilepsy is the real kicker.
Derecho that can knock out power—
though only for a few minutes—violet heat
lightning that can transpire in an hour,
a week, five years, never. I'll skip
the electrocution, please, but keep the rain—
the reservoirs are running low. Grogginess
follows like fog scarfing Douglas firs
at daybreak. But there are problems more
pressing than one person's rather minor
maladies. The aforementioned drought, yes,
screwing the ice caps on tight, keeping
rage and rifles on separate riverbanks.
A colleague once told me I have eight
seconds to hold someone's attention
before it wanders. If so, I'll gladly release
you, kind stranger, to your own concerns.
But won't you look once more? Cliff
vertebrae dynamite into the sea, blighted
pine needles pelt their own sheltering bark.

ADONIS

Before I shared about my ailments,
she figured I'd had an easy life:
popular, carefree, getting by on
an aquiline jawline, an aqueous gaze.
Like Adonis. It reminded me of
the friend in high school art class
who said, *You could play Adonis,*
hiding her blush behind her brush.
The acrylic auburn horses were
a wilderness reborn from her wrist.
But I am no lord, dying and rising
again. No alluring youth, desired
by a pantheon. I should have told
them. We all get gored by mirrors
when we're alone. I'm just as lost,
inchoate, feeble, bewildered as you.
Just as thrumming, as resplendent.

PILLARS OF LIGHT, HILLS OF WHITE

White Sands National Park, New Mexico

The rain doesn't stop us   from dashing up
     and down   the gypsum dunes,

pale as moonlight.   Tufts of soaptree yucca plants
are quietly building   a strong inner life
     as the sands slide around them,

and when we finally rest   on the crest of a hill,
     the San Andres mountains
                 roil and rise

beyond the blanketing clouds.   Then,
     a gash of gold.   An opening.
A tripod of ethereal beams descends   like the legs

of a module come from somewhere   higher
and farther away,   come   to place honey
     on the tips   of our tongues.

Silence is not akin to absence,   though a sunset's

infinitesimal hue change   is the shift from
     alienation   to relation,   emptiness
to fullness, dearth to   abundance.

     The dunes and folds of clouds
have much to teach,   as do the pillars of golden light

gently reaching down,   so I listen,
the reflecting kernels of sand   grainy and cool
     beneath my arms.

TO WHICH WE ARE GOING

John 6:16-21

The story goes something like this:
Capernaum was yet a long way off,
and their shoulders ached from rowing,
weak light bleeding out of the dusk
until only the spectral moon illumined
the waves, tumultuous and writhing
like sea monsters, driving them back
two miles for every one as despair set in
like night. Hours later, terror gusted
through their chests like the squall—
the ghost they'd glimpsed had soaked
hair that clung to his cheeks like kelp,
and he'd walked on the surface of the sea
as one would splash through a puddle.
Peter thought the waterline on his tunic
was too high, then not high enough, John's
mind still racing as those sandals touched
sodden wood—and instantly the boat
was at the land to which they were going.

And that's where it ends. Talk about
a cliffhanger. The walking on water bit
gets all the attention while the teleportation
is hardly mentioned, as if the existence
of one miracle precludes the need for another.
But my days are filled with phenomena
I flounder to explain, pairs of realities
I've neither imagined nor deserved,
one story always leaning into the next.

How the *achiote carnitas* tacos
from La Mulita Express #2 food truck

last week were generously garnished
with both cilantro and lime; how in a month
both a low-hanging, smoldering bead of sun
and a nascent crescent will share the sky's vast
dome; how in two years the turbulent passions
of Verdi's *Il trovatore* will surge from both
the unseen orchestra pit and the opera
singers strutting upon the stage.

There's the knock at the door, and the friend
framed behind it; the slow arc of the tinfoil
wave, and the mullet leaping from
its foamy crest; the crackle of the car radio,
and the wildflowers waiting around the bend.

I admit every stone I've ever tossed
has plummeted beneath the bay's briny skin.
My words have often fallen flat, too rarely
have they revived a friend's flagging spirit.
No one has ever taken me by the hand
and whisked me to the future I am heading to.

But I'm not asking for revelation.
I don't need to be taken anywhere,
don't wish the scroll of my days
unfurled and dissected. I welcome
the breeze rolling off the ridge
into sky the color of spring.
I turn to face the pine-lined trail
to which I am going and set off
on two resolved legs, forging ahead
with the first, and then the other.

THE WINDOW, ONE NOON

Morning was a maqui berry smear
over the bay, that thumb of water where
citizens wailed aboard *La Esmeralda*.
To live on this margin of Earth is to be
adrift. Where can one ground oneself?
My twin has fallen in love thousands
of miles away, but my lovers are alleys
on the next hill twined in clotheslines.
I could read a page of still, stale words—
or dash down for an empanada (or two).
Teenagers jostle on the sidewalk, the girls'
skirts swilling in the briny breeze. A man
laden with groceries hollers, laughing,
to a friend at the corner minimarket.
The woman on the terrace across
the street paints acrylic scenes for tourists
and neighbors. I will join them. I will
join them all.

MEDITATION ON THE STREET ART OF
VALPARAÍSO, CHILE

> *Valparaíso, / how absurd you are … you haven't /*
> *combed your hair, / you've never / had / time to get dressed, /*
> *life / has always / surprised you.*
> —Pablo Neruda, "Oda a Valparaíso"

One hundred-fifty years ago, men hauled buckets of leftover paint
from the port up the city's hills, slathering thick dyes on walls
as they ascended, those houses like hulls protecting precarious lives.

Today, Valparaíso rambles and throbs, shouting with color
as dwellings of turquoise, salmon, periwinkle, peach, and lime
cling to the hillsides through sheer stubbornness. The city

is a street art mecca, every wall an invitation to say something,
anything, the art by turns absurd, obscene, whimsical, provocative,
surreal, yearning—by turns human, in other words. Each afternoon

I set out, aiming to be aimless, so my eyes can be open
to the tiny *abuelita* struggling with her groceries, teenagers
in school uniforms atop Plazuela San Luis sketching the skyline

for an art class, balding Italo Olivarez hobbling into St. Paul's
to play the century-old organ. Scents wash over me like waves:
buttery *empanadas de pino* and sugary *manjar alfajores* wafting

from the open door of a bakery; packs of wandering, sodden dogs;
whiffs of salty ocean spray on the breeze. Sounds ricochet all
around: the screech and clatter of buses careening down narrow

tangles of roads, jovial mutterings of neighbors bartering
in the markets, mellow peals from a cathedral belfry, disgruntled
horns of barges in the bay, the wild cawing of gulls, a young

woman whistling as she ambles along the sloping sidewalk.
So much around me can't speak—*espino* trees, tarnished *ascensor*
rails, cobblestone streets, metal garage doors of storefronts—

while here we are given the miracle of speech, yet we seal our lips
while lying next to lovers, we withhold praise, we avert our gaze
as strangers pass by. These walls, on the other hand, have much

to say: on one, a drunk *porteño* rests by a fire with a dog, pipe,
and empty bottle; on another, fish creatures with human eyes
and legs; on yet another, a wooden cross wears a suit and tie

with a clock's hours—3, 6, 9, 12—marking where the beams
stretch out. Or there's the elderly woman against a pink background,
her bun tight and fingers thrumming on the sidewalk's chipped edge;

the flight of stairs draped in piano keys. On one wall, a woman's
huge, green, pixelated face, rainbow liquid spilling from her open
mouth; and farther down, a man clenches a blue octopus' tentacle

in his teeth. There are the turquoise and violet tones of two dream-
like figures emblazoned across a ten-story apartment building;
and the tiny cartoonish outline of a bespectacled man pouring

a watering pail on the side of concrete steps, as if tending
the grass. Wandering this unkempt city, doubting my grasp
of the native tongue, I often retreat within myself. I have been

invited into silence's lonely home. Yet I always smile at the sight
of the ardent but amiable declaration, "We are not hippies, we are
happies" scrawled in white against a kaleidoscopic mosaic half-

way up Cerro Alegre. As if the art knows it's more than its colors,
more than the hard surfaces it was born onto. Buses clatter down
the hills, gulls caw, bells peal, and the walls ramble all the while.

C BOARDING GROUP

The gate attendant jokes
he's saved the best for last,
like in Cana when guests
tasted the best in the last hour
and two thousand years later
we still can't fathom such
a shrug of generosity.
When was the last time
we spoke with our neighbors
down the street? And what
can't a son trace back to his
mother? Mine wept as I flew
two thousand miles away
to sizzling *parrillada*, *vino tinto*,
chalky canyons, freezing rapids.
As we all link arms on the rim
of the raft, the stranger's hair
soaked and eyes sunshot,
our shoulders cool to the other's
touch, we are transmuted into
a speeding O down the throat
of the land's untapped desire—
afterwards, as we change
back into dry clothes
in the hostel, I have no need
for a miracle, for wine to be
anything but malbec, for
water to be anything but river.

END OF THE WORLD

Monte Olivia, Ushuaia, Argentina

Snow-husked and salient, the eon-carved
mountain is now a tooth tip-dipped in rosewater
as dusk baptizes with passion

> *Agostini: The pedestal of this fantastic mountain castle,*
> *with gigantic strong walls, covered with armor of ice,*
> *exceeded by haunting spires that are able to seduce …*

three years before he surmounts her,
the missionary-mountaineer arrives
in Tierra del Fuego, this land of fire,
land of smoke, land of names

Beagle Channel, Murray Narrows, Strait of Magellan
Onashaga, Yah'ga-Asha'ga, Onaisín

> *Darwin: The language of these people, according to*
> *our notions, scarcely deserves to be called articulate.*
> *Captain Cook has compared it to a man clearing his throat …*

YHWH or Geova, Temáukel or Watauinéiwa,
how many mouths have tried to pronounce
the unsayable, the encompassing?

One language can't tell the whole story,
try as it might to silence other tongues
Already my English has lost the drift

And what then when a word-carrier dies?
Ángela Loij, Selk'nam, 1974
Cristina Calderón, Yahgan, 2022

If a calamity is the "fin del mundo,"
the sign carved for tourists is positing a truth

> *Bridges: The natives ... have received dreadful provocation ...*
> *it is ruinous for them to attempt retaliation for spears, arrows*
> *and stones cannot compete with Winchester rifles ...*

Through the cacophony of cawing gulls,
seals lounging on seaweed-strewn stones
below the red-and-white lighthouse recall

Yahgan bodies painted with ocher, charcoal,
white clay, slathered with seal fat for heat
as families gathered around fires in bark canoes,

sharing stories and shucked limpets when apparitions
of European vessels hulked from the windswept
underworld, imposing on the day's unwritten history

> *Agostini: But the most imposing attraction is Monte*
> *Fitz Roy ... He is lord of all this vast*
> *mountainous region, he is another Cervino ...*

lords of themselves those families were,
at least six thousand years into some beginning,
while in the blue haze above me now

a V of cormorants sharp as Olivia's anointed peak
serrates the sky at the end of this world

AN ISLAND IN THE CENTER OF ANOTHER WORLD

Salar de Uyuni, Bolivia

The black rocks beneath my boots and poles of cacti
next to me ember while the entrancing expanse

of bright white scales reaches to the pink ribbon
of mountains off to the side in the distance,

and to the rest of the hard horizon, above which sky
yellows upward by degrees into a loosening gold,

then a pearly silver, then the most delicate of blues.
Standing atop Isla Incahuasi, our guide explains

the salt flats we see spilling out in all directions go on
for ten thousand square kilometers, and this island

is all that remains of an ancient volcano that was
submerged up to forty thousand years ago. As if numbers,

beyond a certain point, signify anything. As if this view
is more astounding than the journey it took to get here:

three days crammed into a Jeep with six strangers,
the surreal sea-colored mountains pointing the way,

the blinding sand and sky shimmering and shifting
around us. In the unvoiced awkwardness of people

rubbing elbows when they can't even remember
each other's nations or names, we spent hours gazing

out at the gleaming vastness, anticipating, knowing
the hour would come when we'd be here. Like

a polished brown lucuma seed, the pulsing muscly
twist of a heart, a doused planet, the crumble

of a long-dead volcanic cone—all improbable, yet
all existing, just so, in the center of something.

CONJUNCTIONS

> *We don't get back / those days we don't caress, don't make love*
> —Jim Harrison "Letters to Yesenin, #21"

In the hostel courtyard, the Israeli girl
and I spoke in Spanish for hours, laughing
when an *abuelita* asked if we were *pololeando*

> June 17, 2 BC
> .1 degree

When she stripped off her sweaty clothes
in the shared bunk room, I averted my stare,
avoided the sin of skin, of bare want

> July 24, 366 AD
> .5 degrees

At dusk, we passed each other on the dusty
street—what words were exchanged?—but
I foolishly followed my belly to a bowl
of desert *quinoto* instead

> November 16, 605 AD
> .8 degrees

Late that night, the astronomy tour guide
texted: *I hear there's a break in the clouds*
so he and I barreled down the scything road,
past barren ridges and curupiric crags

> August 20, 961 AD
> .7 degrees

Venus and Jupiter smoldered as one entity,
reminiscent of the time they clasped into
retrograde motion above Bethlehem

October 13, 1352 AD
.4 degrees

We skidded off the tongue of black asphalt
licking the refinery lights of distant Calama
as the glowing orbs overhead ached to fuse

January 1, 1783 AD
.6 degrees

Knee-deep in gravel, a penitent poet
with an eye to a viewfinder, who am I
to speak of two planets feeling anything?
Of their metallic cores attracting desire?

June 30, 2015 AD
.3 degrees

To seem so near, passing in the night,
to be five hundred-fourteen million miles
away from ever touching the other.

ALERCE TREES

The alerce trees I hike among
are more than three thousand years old,
younger than the volcanoes the locals

promised me a view of, but older
than any other living thing I've seen.
I imagine them strong and content

as halfway around the globe, David
gazes from his roof at Bathsheba,
caught somewhere between stimulus

and response, twirling his crown
of gemstones, then setting it aside,
all while the trees I walk past on this

Chilean ridge are transpiring, greeting
the morning sun without complaint, with
no need for strategy or rules or theology.

If we could tap into their memories,
what do they not have mouths to say,
what do we not have ears to hear?

I've forgotten most of my life, though
perhaps the fact that I can remember
anything at all should be pondered with

gratitude. Still, many of the moments
I hoped to savor are gone, while plenty
of humdrum scenes in nameless days

are tucked safely away, clear, nearly
violent in their detail. As I hike
among that solitude of soil and branch

and leaf, those grand trees lifting up
the afternoon, I sense the buoyant emptiness
of all I've still yet to experience, of all

the blessings I've yet to be given. How
could I know that later in the year, I'll
crane my neck for an hour as the sun

sinks somewhere in a Bolivian desert,
trying to memorize an unbroken field
of clouds burning blood red across

the entire sky; or that I'll gaze for
the first time at the bare curve of a lover's
back, the soft arc a fiddle's body,

the skin taut and vibrating like strings
ready to be drawn across; or that I'd
drive with her down a road out West,

snaking through an aspen-gold valley
while on either side of us mountains—
that existed eons before these alerce

trees—open upward to the sky; that
we would feel old and young, lost yet
found as the miles slid beneath us,

as we forged ahead, hearts also opening
to stem and stone, and sky. What words
would we exchange like precious gems?

IV

DUST STORMS MAY EXIST

Tearing through the agave and ocotillo
desert scrub of southern New Mexico,
two road signs blur past: First,
"Alkali welcomes you. Eat beef."
Then, the second: "Dust storms may exist."

I nearly swerved from the blacktop.
Please no, I thought. *Not another one.*
Not another existential crisis
or metaphysical quandary. I have
enough of those already, plenty
of ghosts flitting across my vision
like tumbleweeds. *Am I a good
man? What happens when we die?
Does God exist, and, if so, which one?*
If dust storms do, in fact, exist,
I hope they're not like hurricanes—
battering barrages of wind,
obliterating time and memory; not like
maelstroms of saltwater, dragging
bedraggled mariners to their deaths.
I hope, instead, they're like hands
scouring wooden furniture with
sandpaper until smooth, like rivers
polishing millennia of stone, like
a hundred-thousand whetstones
sharpening iron until it gleams.
I hope each storm has an eye,
an expansive, intimate place
where both my body and soul
can draw skyward, buoyed,
suspended in the air like a word.

A FACE IN THE MIRROR

I'd promised her the canyon would live up to its name,
be beyond grand, yet here we were: our view impeded

by the zoo of people clamoring for selfies, the colors
washed out by the noonday sun, shaking our heads

at a sign urging us not to feed the squirrels for risk
of spreading plague. It turns out wildness is not a thing

to be grasped. In this space, I take off a layer of time
and am a year younger, hiking down Bright Angel Trail

with my brother as we approach a bend and come face
to face with two suntanned women. Southern courtesy

compels me to step out of the way, toward the edge, but
the dirt is loose beneath my boots, my ankle quivering—

then his hand hard on my shoulder as he yanks me away
from danger. A hand is a parachute, a brother a face

in the mirror. We make it to the bottom, sweaty and aching,
and live a week on rafts, the world above wisping into memory.

On the water, swallows swoop and dart like dogfighters,
a mile of cinnamon-red rock looms above us, the river churns

like an earthen engine. On the water, the only direction is
forward; upon hitting a roiling rapid, the only choice is through.

Within the motion, a stillness; within the heat, a refuge;
within the current, all the paths we'll pass by and clearings

we'll amble across, all the glances and gestures we'll share
like canteens, all the sentences we'll ever think to say.

HEAT LIGHTNING

Seventy miles from Moab
she grew silent in the passenger seat
as we saw the sky burgeon
with dark blue thunderheads,
watched them metastasize as
the last light drained into a thin line
of fire on the horizon

The vastness of the storm outstripped
the desert flung on either side of us
as we hurtled through the night,
lightning veining sideways
in the distance

Earlier in the road trip
we failed to stop at that chapel
in Sedona, the one that juts out
from the coppery butte like a fossil,
proving it's possible to belong
somewhere

This morning our wordless surprise as we
lay braided in the bedroom's black canyon,
her face cradled in the crook of my arm

Now, in this moment, I want
to have something to say, wish
she would speak, as stormclouds
obscure every fiery freckle of stars
and the synapses of lightning
blossom into an orange-violet glow
where the road vanishes

Perhaps it's not too much
of a stretch to say:
The universe is a cathedral of sorts,
an ocean of oxygen, carbon, energy,
but mostly
darkness, space—
like the blind exhalation
before prayer

OVERPOPULATION

If every tree in Eden had been
permitted, wouldn't our curse
have been to live forever?

WORDS SPOKEN WITH TENDERNESS

Language: my country / where light /
rhymes with night / death / with breath—
—Franz Wright, "Language My Country"

If even one letter were blotted from this page,
if a single jot or tittle were askew, the moment
would be impoverished. I find myself in an old

cathedral whose ceiling resembles the underside
of an overturned ship, without a buttressing truss
but slathered with trust that what we see is being

held together, invisibly. Which is sturdier:
a beam of wood or a word spoken with
tenderness? Shadows angle down the sloped

sill like a country road diverted to avoid
a flour mill. A little leaven causes a loaf to rise,
but we've learned rocketing through the sky

gets us no closer to an unmapped heaven.
This stone enclosure, drafty and vacant
as a tomb, sits silent. Or perhaps it's pregnant

as a womb, humming with the potentialities
of all the lives that will pass through these
pews, even once, in the unfolding centuries.

I used to think sunlight sifting through stained
glass was evidence everything is illuminated,
or would be in time. But is it a creation or

a cremation, the ball of unseen nuclear fusion
deep within our sun that transfigures elements,
radiates blinding heat and light atom by atom,

hand over hand? The swirling plasma surface's
inferno tears through the vacuum of space
for millions of miles before bursting benevolently

through this window as wave-particle rays. They
hover around me, oblique yet palpable, landing
softly as whispers on my still, upturned face.

NIGHT WEIGHT

There's no other way to say it:
We're lost.

Retracing our steps for the fourth time,
the sun long since extinguished behind
the escarpments, we find ourselves

in the same rocky intersection as before.
As we clamber over boulders, squeeze

through crevasses in the desert landscape,
I think of the trail mix crumbs and water bottle
in my backpack, measuring the chill

on my face, wondering:
Could we really survive the night?

Odds were: yes. And of course,
we'd been lost plenty of times before.

Three hundred miles to the southwest
and a few weeks younger, I'd wound us
up a steep cliff side, slipping around

shadowy statues of deer before realizing
we were on the wrong road. Once back

at ground level and on the right one, the night's
darkness was too deep, too implacable.
We crept along the dusty caliche

at a snail's pace, our headlights revealing
chalky rock and brush before

dissolving into the inky emptiness that stretched up
    to a fingernail of moon illuminating only
        the most threadbare rag of cloud.

    Miles led to monstrous cows glaring at us
        in the middle of the road. When they

finally moved, I got out to read a sign, only for cactus barbs
    to claw my calves, only to find the words eroded
        from the metal and from our throats

    as frigid fear gripped us as tightly as she
        held the wheel. Two months

of road-tripping, and this was the first instant
    I realized it was actually possible to die
        in the desert, to simply disappear

    into the night like a dream. Nothing spoke save
        the wheels grinding on until

a red-eyed rabbit blocked our passage, zig-zagging
    to spite us as lights appeared in the rearview,
        a lone truck baring down,

    the murderer in this dime-store story. We couldn't
        run the rabbit over—though we may be

killed we will not kill—so we sank off to the shoulder
    to let the truck whoosh by in a tunnel of gravel
        and dust. Just then, a side road, a sign:

    Our campsite emerged, and relieved laughter mixed
    with margarita mix and campfire glow—

... Prone to wander, Lord, I feel it,
prone to leave the God I love—

I'm jolted back to our present predicament
      by the off-key echo of an 18th-century hymn.
          The voices, though earnest, were failing

      to coalesce, but the night's cape was torn.
          We pass the group of worshippers;

hands point the way, the trail flattens out,
      the parking lot comes into view,
          the road snakes back to Moab.

      Later, at Miguel's Baja Grill, we clasp
          hands across the table over plates

of sopping enchiladas suizas, smiling so much
      it hurts, the physicality of relief as surging
          as the adrenaline pulse of terror.

She admits her stomach had sunk upon hearing
      the hymn—*damned to hell after all*, she joked—

but belief was beside the point. As it rippled out
      that song had been a sacrament sweeter
          than wine, an ember the void of night

      could not quench, the sound from those lungs
          reminding us what's lost is nothing

      to what's found.

ADDITIONAL QUESTIONS FOR THE CANYON

for Jesse Graves and William Wright

Why are you so silent?
> *I'd rather think than speak. Your own words are the babbling of a brook.*

What have you seen?
> *I have watched ages pass and species disintegrate like clouds.*

Do you hear outlaw country music ricocheting off your walls and gorges?
> *Not as often as I hear echoes of the ancient sea that once engulfed me.*

So, you're aware of erosion?
> *My youth was ripped from me as yours was from you. Time refines us all.*

What does it feel like when hikers amble along the trails carved into your skin?
> *Like ants scrabbling over your arm, I suppose. Like remnants of raindrops.*

Do you remember everyone who's ever descended into your depths?
> *You'd be surprised how much even one soul weighs. I forget nothing.*

What about those who merely photographed you from your edges?
> *Most are mist to me, though a few cross my mind every century or so.*

What's it like in the heat of the summer sun?
> *A surrender. A shedding of inhibition. An opening of self.*

And the cold hardness of winter?
> *A noiseless howl that would deafen you if you stayed with me.*

Does anything stay with you?
> *Patter of pronghorn hoof, grip of piñon root, sorrowful caress of wind.*

Does any human ever really know you?
> *I've never been more exposed, but I have secrets hidden away still.*

Do you ever get lonely?
> *I am always alone.*

PHOTOGRAPH OF MY FATHER IN A TARNISHED
SILVER FRAME, 1999

In the bruise of a cloudy afternoon,
I noticed, perhaps for the first time,
a picture among the miniature
ceramic boxes and knickknacks
on the bookshelf. Those pools of blue
seemed surprised and amused
as the crest of his brown hair broke
and tumbled over his forehead, his
smile stretching through the canyons
in his cheeks, and for a moment—
I thought I heard something that
sounded like his laugh, although
I had never heard it before.

DEAD HORSES

Dead Horse Point, Utah

Thousands of feet below us, a horseshoe
of river encircles a hoof of reddened rock.

The overlook gets its name from this view,
where, according to legend, wild mustangs

were corralled on the slender mesa top, then
culled by cowboys. One time, a century or so

ago, the narrow neck of land was left fenced
off with brush, and the broomtails died

of thirst within sight of the Colorado River
meandering two thousand feet below them.

Beyond the point that bore the weight
of those bleached bones, rusty strata sink

and rise as they stretch into the distance.
An hour ago, we'd gotten word her sister's baby

was on the way, and now we let the spacious
silence swell with hope. Above us to one side,

the sun melts into streaks of currant jam,
to the other a full moon climbs into

the sky, and then a comet blazes smack dab
between them, a spiraling fireball.

The spectrum of the spectacle is immense,
and I'm struck by the thought that so much

is beginning, so much expiring, with us
multitude of travelers suspended in the middle

of it all, somewhere between a child inhaling
its first breath and a comet's tail petering out.

As light fades and the landscape purples
and blurs above the severed citadels

of plateaus, the plummeting flood basins,
I think how we're all galloping toward

the edges of what we've envisioned, tumbling
into the unknown. Next to me, she has

become a pensive silhouette, and I look past
her, down to the protruding point, wondering

if horses really did die out there, or if it's
just another wisp of myth on a western wind.

If so, we're often like those stranded creatures—
everything in sight, what we need so far away.

THE LONG LIGHT OF LATE AFTERNOON

Either the universe is perpetually silent
       or it is always shouting, and if the latter,
what on earth is it saying?

     I suppose I'm being presumptuous when I have
my ears cocked only for 21st century American English,
       with a whisper of a southern drawl.

     Perhaps I was given an answer years ago,
       or a better question, but distance
or inattentiveness muffled the sound.

     Now, a teal butterfly wings through the oleander
as the long light of late afternoon slants over switchgrass,
       then darts in a flash of blue down

     to the river bend. Any revelation there
       might have been goes unsaid, waits
to be revealed some other time.

     In the meantime, earthworms tunnel
iron-flecked soil, basketballs ricochet off suburban
       backboards, black holes

     wheel through dark matter as they swallow
       galaxies, particles of the sinking sun sift
softly past kitchen windows.

     I've learned not to pore over the map
too long, to instead keep my eyes peeled for the bridge
       that's—as sure as eggs—up ahead.

INVENTORY OF PIT STOPS

Grime on a concrete overpass
gleams as rain spits and foams

while shipping containers
loiter in a vacant railyard.

A weedy gas station clings,
obsolete, to a gravel county road

like an ulcer, silent as
a Louisiana casino slated for

demolition. Not your reality,
you say, nor mine, but plenty

of invisible things are true:
quarks, black holes, loneliness.

Where can a man get a cup
of coffee in the sibilating night?

The Shonto Trading Post
crouches against the red

flesh of the earth, selling bracelets,
baskets, handspun rugs, sodas

that will jitter the nerves
of the placeless. So sink into

the dissolved lithium gurgling
from the Uncompahgre,

find the tranquility the water
promises. Pacify yourself in

the nude hot springs, strip yourself
of sanity, certainty, illusory

notions. Perch like the black cat
on the white F-150 at Jay Bros,

staring like the black and white
of our politics ladled over polite

conversation. This the land
of barbeque ribs on red trays,

soda in Styrofoam cups, crucifixions
of power lines carrying mycelia

of light across the switchboard
of America. One wire fizzes out,

one fluorescent bulb above
a greasy fuel pump flickers.

A spark flashes, a spruce ignites,
an entire landscape is aflame.

ORBITAL

Though the vistas and fossils are magnetizing
us to Badlands National Park, the refrain pulses
We don't have time. We don't, we don't

go, but we do fuel up at Jay Bros in the middle
of nowhere Nebraska, gorging ourselves
on coconut chicken and garlic naan inside,

laughing as we laughed over jerky and tangerines
after ascending the museum's stairs in Flagstaff
to discover Tony Norris, a leather-vested Merlin,

gesticulating cowboy poetry, crooning about
a long-lost blue bandana. Such speckled radiance.
Why can't we be more like century-old saguaros:

wise, waving a greeting, offering a hug goodbye?
Tomorrow, a placard will tell me Black Elk once said,
Some moments in a man's life remember themselves

and I wonder if this evening is such an event,
the elements of gas and food becoming remnants,
so though time tumbles on, their imprints remain.

The days stack up, the minutes tick down,
ancient ammonites and stone staircases spiral
ever downward, ever upward, ever inward,

further and farther, faster, until the absolute
locus of focus is so close, so infinitesimal,
it lies a field away and cannot be seen at all.

TO THE MEN WHO LAUGHED AT MOSES

And to the kids who made fun of their classmate after
school yesterday when he stuttered while trying

to tell a joke. Plenty of things are perforated, after all:
the jungle gym rungs, the white lines bisecting

a desert road, the stories we tell ourselves. Every
moment has its antecedents. The crowd gathering,

the tangling of meanings, the puncture of stony stares.
What if the prophet's mother had done as she was told?

I've no quarrel with guidelines; I'm thankful for
the trees lining the road, the rocks along the riverbank.

But do you remember what you were doing when
you realized rules really were made to be broken?

Show me the person who prefers obedience over
openness, and I'll show you last evening's sunset—

singular, though no more or less brilliant than
the billion before it. Still, the cumulus clouds reveled

in the beams, coating themselves in turmeric and sumac,
unpretentious, but flushed with naked magnificence.

I often wonder what would change if we cared less
about being right and more about being made right.

No matter if it comes slowly, haltingly, without fanfare.
Consider the aged cedar whose trunk continues to swell

imperceptibly, despite the phantom limb some punk
broke off in boredom, despite its lightly charred

crown from last year's wildfire. That sort of strength
doesn't wait for a break in the chatter, a break in

the water. A night heron rises from the river like a memory
about to return, skims the reeds as it sets its course

for the day when words come easily, when the young
man on the shore knows what it's like to be free.

WHEN A COUNTRY IS A METAPHOR

One could make the case that more than
anything else, this country is a road.

Not a verdigris statue in a harbor, nor
a rusty canyon plummeting a mile into

the earth, not as much as a black ribbon
of asphalt baking in June's hazy heat.

This road unrolls across flung plains,
winds through cedar forests, plunges

into chalky deserts, ascends obsidian
mountains. It proceeds from gritty

victories, past colossal failures, toward
hope in a five-year-old's eyes.

It passes cheery small towns, ramshackle
steel mills, tangles of light-studded

metropolises, circles so many decent
people trying their best to make a living

and make love and take kind steps toward
their neighbors. The texture of this road

shifts with every town and turn and mile;
it isn't tied to the past, but it hasn't

forgotten where it came from; it doesn't
fear the future, but it hasn't yet arrived.

Flying down such a highway, I am
unfettered from everything stationary,

even my own past, am as malleable
as a ridgeline curve, able to divert course

or press the pedal of longing down so far
I rocket toward the seam of horizon,

beyond even its infinite edge. Yet as
I sense this seeming endlessness can't

be truly endless, I glance over at her—
and one deep breath later we're belting out

a David Allan Coe tune in unison, swaying
and smiling, the windows rolled down

letting steel guitar jangle out past brown
towers of Iowa corn soaked in the blue

and sun and clouds that are here now
and won't be here again, pavement rumbling

beneath the tires, the world outside
rushing by, the sky and stalks and song

drenched in gladness, going on forever.

V

A SEA STREWN GENEROUSLY

Priesthoods and beasthoods, sombers and glees ...
—Christian Wiman, "All My Friends Are Finding New Beliefs"

Just beyond the edge of dusk's cold kiln,
a startle of starlings over the ashen river,
black peppercorns against an eggplant sky,
incandescent without ever intending to be.

Scriptures and strictures, hallows and hollows, the tangible throb—

A woman with a cross atop her blouse
bellows blades outside the abortion clinic,
a man wearing a teal turban buys an extra
maakouda for the beggar at the corner.

Harm or harmony—toward which will religion swerve?—

Meanwhile, an axolotl grins shyly,
green moss perches on parched bark,
softly spiked virions float aimlessly,
get sucked into an unsuspecting lung.

This land a sea strewn generously with marvels and perils—

The jagged blue clefts of glacier ice,
the tomato hue of an altiplano laguna,
a stranger with lavender hair passing,
pennies glistening on the pavement.

Inspiration and aspiration, all we look upon and do not see—

A friend turns my way, the screen
in my hand weightless and worthless.
After all these years, I'm still startled
when I hear my name uttered by another.

HIGHWAYS LIKE FROZEN RIVERS

The highways like frozen rivers
          isolate,
capillaries and deltas of asphalt
                    sprawl,
This is the future, the past will say.

The roads fill with travelers almost
          together
yet always alone, infinite headlights
                    weave
and merge—why is it still dark?

There you are, driven insane by
          clogged
arteries of pavement and pollution,
                    gasping,
a human out of air, for some joy.

Friend, breathe deeply. It helps.
          Can you see
beyond the windshield, the mountains?
                    Can you hear
above the radio, the rain?

SUNLIGHT, A JUBILATION

Bicycling down the city street,
breathless with light
breaking through the trees
and pooling on the ground,
dark-dappled radiance,
heat of the rays in our eyes
and on our skin as I try
to understand the brightness
of it all—this the same sunlight
that poured into the canyon
when I was just a boy
and had not yet begun to worry
about the economy or the future,
simply amazed to be alive,
my panting lungs thirsting
for wind that tastes like spring
water, my sight for corporate
buildings next to me to become
a limestone cliff crested with
cedars ablaze in a green ecstasy—
the sunlight drenches me,
eleven years old again:
seeing promises in the branches,
rustlings of romance in the leaves,
loss in the latticed shadows,
summer sun in everything.

STATE OF BEING

Both so nervous that first night
we shared a bed,

the first night I'd shared a bed with anyone

so I powered on my tablet and read some
Steinbeck, you know the passage:

and now that you don't have to be
perfect, you can be good

and good lord the ease that encircled us

for we were just friends who liked literature
and learning and had hit the road together

as one does if one has privilege and time
and, say, there was that one day

—

in some tiny Tennessee town
where a bearded man in pressed Civil War attire
gestured toward a Confederate flag

beyond which sat eight stone hearts, each
the size of a calf, emblazoned with the words:

Prepare to meet God, with instructions
on the nearest to *erect on Jupiter 1990-S*

as if extraterrestrials would comprehend
hearts engraved in English

—

or when we filled our hearts and bellies
in an old car repair shop in Ozona, Texas

where a woman with a gap-toothed grin and
penetrating glare served up heaping portions

of barbeque brisket, pinto beans, coleslaw,
cornbread, lemonade, and as we took
our leave

I thanked her husband for the meat, to which
he silently tipped his dusty hat

—

and that older woman who sidled up
to me on the dingy dance floor
of the Buffalo Chip Saloon in Tucson

teaching me to waltz with a vise grip,
steering my hips and telling me

how she once saw
beetles so big you could rope and ride 'em
and what do you say to that?

what does one say to the chopped hair
of Chiricahua Apaches in the exhibit
the next day,

strewn about as if the museum floor
was a hair salon for crying out loud

—

and I wonder how loudly those
Apache fiddles can resonate, the ones

Anthony Belvado constructed from
agave stalks and horsehair strings,

and farther down, that wall of rusty
thumb pianos and Cape Town ramkies,
dials drilled into Castrol oil cans

back in the car she turned the music up
but we were stuck on the same months-old

playlist, stuck on playing at being lovers

—

how playfully I leaned out the car window
as we left Telluride, the rainbow

behind us so magnificent it was corny

and I kept repeating, *It's right there,*
it's right there! as she drove on and grinned,

the aspens glinting golden up and up

—

and now up in this skyscraper, I know
my massive Lego saber can't save her

and there's no need for a knight
in quick-dry clothes and hiking boots,
no need for a hero of any kind

but I swing anyway, the plastic blocks
crumbling at the first swipe

and later, on the hurtling hearse of the L
train, among the other passengers,

each of us in our separate selves

I'll think it is ok to make eye contact:
the eyes of the terrified beseech

—

to the east, bees whirl and whorl around
calico aster blooms on Indiana roadsides

tall ironweed stems and iron forges blast
across the hard billowing plains of Ohio

silos scattered across Pennsylvania
farmland store oats, rye, barley, soybeans
and who can say what else—

but we haven't seen any of that yet
and even when we do, can't
promise I'll know what to make of it all

—

so what should I make of this moment?
or this one?

what state are we in anyway?

what state are we in the midst
of being?

AN EVENING IN TOLEDO, OHIO

Past the muddy river,
  the steel bridge,

   past bristles
of trees already bare with winter's
  approaching,

   past the glass and concrete
of hotels and financial centers,
  flue-gas stacks,

   canopies of power lines,
the sky is a wordless gray:

so much muted, unsaid.

The red circle
  of the setting sun blazes
against the lack of color

as I take a breath of the cigarette
  smoke-swathed air.

Before yesterday, I'd never seen
  those black and white
photographs of my father,

   images of him as a child
    in the hallway

of my aunt's house ten minutes
  to the south of where I stand.

The burning globe
ahead of me, that circle coming

around again, is older
            than it has ever been,
                    as young

            as it will ever be.

FATHER FIGURES

Who counts?

How about   the tee-ball coach   who didn't
    have to   raise his voice   to raise his
standards   or   the Turkish coffee shop owner
        in his rad sunglasses and goatee   who always
    let us win   at chess   whose Caffe Sorbettos
were always   on the house.   Or the firefighter
a coil of laughter   and muscles who   helped us
        lift the leviathan   hose who helped   me
    catch my first fish—   a 20-inch red—
an emanation   of kindness   until
    the slicing curve of pavement   ripped him
from   his motorcycle   in the fall.

Who counts?

Not   the two blips   partnered   to my mom
    for mere months: the mustached man   who
in my memory   resides   in a recliner
cold beer in hand   at two in the   afternoon
        nor the balding banker   counting
on us   not finding out   he was gay and when
    we did   quietly packed his things   and left.
All because   well-intentioned church ladies
        whispered things   like: "Those boys need
a father." Figures.

Who counts?

I'll add the Black man   who managed the family
pine farm   who taught me to   ride a horse
    shoot a rifle   drive a car.   Who chuckled
when I   drove   into a muddy clay ditch

80

and crumpled the passenger side door   like tinfoil.
And my grandfather   like us   in his apron
     and underwear   after   we awoke
from spending the night   the way   his aged
hands   resembled   a mottled version
of my own   as we tenderly kneaded   the dough
   into buttermilk biscuits   needed   each other.
Certainly my surfer   stepdad   who pulled out
   his toolbox and table saw   so we could   build
a platform bedframe   in the garage   him not
     spelling it all out   to speak   instead letting
the whirring   drill drive the point   home.

And let's count   the woman   who every night
   had supper   simmering   on the stove
the elbow of her stirring arm   bearing a dark scar
   where   a pebble embedded   when she shielded
my skull   during a stumble   who decades ago
held an infant   in each arm   hands sure and strong
     as any man's.

THREE MINUTES IN NIJMEGEN

All I recall from that day are shards, fragments.

The rumbling train ride to the eastern city.

Hans' height, the gentle hunch in his back.

Ria's tight hug around my waist, those cerulean eyes
searching my face for any semblance of my father's—

how close they'd all become after he hitched a ride
with their children back in the eighties.

How they had a recording of his voice—would I like
to hear it?—it must be around here somewhere.

My brother and I playing chess with the same
wooden pieces his hands had held. So many moves,
nearly endless possibilities, except the one.

The world beyond the window all
wrought-iron, cloudscape, wine-red brick.

—

Think of all the people in other apartments,
other cities, brewing coffee, reading newspapers,
strumming guitars, sitting on sofas alone.

Or those wandering foreign sidewalks, humming
unfamiliar songs, eyes overcast with want.

What would change if we listened to their stories,
if we gave them a lift to where they were going,
if we invited them into the groves of our dinner tables?

Sons and daughters, all of us. How easy
to see the leaps from stranger to friend to family
are bends along the same road.

—

What would I say to my father if I had
three unhurried minutes?

Perhaps: What did you dream of as a child?
Have you discovered a hidden key that unlocks joy?

Maybe: Is there some prismatic plane from which you
see and know me, smiling at what you see and know?

Or: Can one distinguish between yearning and loneliness
and love, or do they each taste the same?

Love: how saccharine a word in a world where
a child fumbles in a slum for one crumb
to fill her famished belly,

where a three-hundred-year-old pecan tree
is splintered for the real estate clinging to its roots,

where a teenage boy slips into a teeming plaza,
disintegrating himself in a pink bloom in the hope
of taking others with him.

—

Take me back to those three minutes in Nijmegen,
porcelain mugs of tea cooling on the table, forgotten

as Hans and Ria adjust the volume and the cassette
whirs into place with a crackle, an inhale, a voice:

National Eddie Broadcasting System,
one, two, three, four, five. [rustle]

You know, with all the education I thought I had,
this is the third time I've tried to make this tape...

Outside the apartment, a bicycle dings merrily,
neighbors mutter good-naturedly on the sidewalk,
a woodlark flickers past the glass, and I cannot

believe what is happening is happening.

I have tried so many times, too. I am trying still.

TWO DIFFERENT AMERICAS

pass each other as a teenager
in smudged periwinkle dress

and crumpled bonnet scooters
down the county road despite

the 18-wheeler launching a muddy
puddle onto her back. The livestream

glitches as the police chief mentions
the *egregious use of force* and an

unwavering commitment to justice
in the same interview. From the back

stoop, a child clutching an empty can
sees the distant silos of a sugar beet

factory that just wrapped up a month
of record-setting productivity.

A Western Express semi
is technically heading east through

a metropolis's cement tangle,
but trajectories shift. On Sundays,

the country church thrums
like a whale's cavernous belly;

on Mondays, its back wall provides
blessed shelter from icy gusts

for those needing a sip of something
warm or to blow a bit of smoke.

Leaving Lancaster, we stop at an Amish
farm stand, and as the girl rings up

fleshy, sweet heirloom tomatoes,
there is something familiar about

her damp hem, her slate gaze,
her shoulders' firm refusal to fall.

ABANDONED FAIRYTALE

You can't miss it: along US-30, the towering
Pied Piper of Hamelin, patriotic
in his red pants, blue jacket and cap,
golden instrument pressed to his lips—

> *From street to street he piped, advancing /*
> *And step for step, they followed, dancing*

But the fairytale park has been closed
for decades, the rest of the giant statues—
the goofy pink egg atop a stone wall,
the whale with a knight on its tongue,
the brown shoe (conveniently roofed),
the mushroom with a door and chimney,
as if someone resides in the stipe—
are dingy, deteriorating. So much
abandoned, left in the past.

> *There was an old woman who lived in a shoe, /*
> *She had so many children she didn't know*
> *what to do*

What to do with the ten thousand miles
behind us, with the hundred or so left to go?
Do we continue to merge like streams,
or do we diverge, disentangle, drift apart
like tides until years utterly obscure
the other from view?

> *Simple Simon went a-fishing / For to catch*
> *a whale: / All the water he had got /*
> *Was in his mother's pail*

While a sack of pale scenes dangles
at my side, the flayed light simmers
out of the sky and I'm back in Memphis,
sequined pants sparkling on an animatronic
Elvis; back in Arizona, the dusty shoes
of Japanese internment camp prisoners
stacked like bones; back in North
Platte, the Buffalo Bill Cody shrine
jutting from the Nebraskan flatness,
wooden and phallic.

> *Humpty Dumpty sat on a wall, /*
> *Humpty Dumpty had a great fall*

We drive on, past cracked Schellsburg
storefront windows, empty and eerie,
past all those museums we'd perused
glimpsing ourselves reflected back
in the panes of glass. Everything
after tonight will be remembering
a remembering. The mind recalls
itself, recollecting what cannot
be collected again.

> *Old Mother Goose, when /*
> *She wanted to wander, / Would—*

PRECARIOUS CAIRNS

First it was about the sights I was seeing, then
who I was seeing them with. The land itself,
then the sensation of soaring far above it.

First it was about music, history, geography,
regional cuisine and lore, then simply
an adventure shared with a girl, a friend.

So much has been given and received:
conversations, months, bodies—
the precarious cairns of memory.

A year from now, the slim spire of the Sentinel
hoodoo will succumb to eons of erosion,
collapsing like beliefs that once held us intact.

There will be no witnesses to its vanishing.
Thousands will scour photo albums for proof
it had been there, evidence they had too—

as will I, finding none. I didn't record
our discussion with the young Navajo guide
at Antelope Canyon, the reasons for our mutual

interest in one another already blurring away.
I can't replicate the recipe for Adobe Deli's
cheesy onion soup. I didn't jot down

the bawdy tunes and clever poems amassed
from descendants of settlers on spiral-bound
sheaves in the Luna Mimbres Museum.

A few tendrils of knowledge, of truth,
have yet to be pressed into a page, a song.
It has taken me so long to be inside my own life.

NOTES

The dates and degrees of Venus and Jupiter conjunctions in "Conjunctions" were calculated by Scott Perkins, PhD, on Stellarium software.

The quotes in "End of the World" are taken from Father Alberto María de Agostini in the article https://www.patagonia-argentina.com/en/father-de-agostini/, Charles Darwin's *The Voyage of the Beagle*, and Thomas Bridges' *A Short Account of Tierra del Fuego and Its Inhabitants*.

The structure of "Additional Questions for the Canyon" owes itself to the poem "Questions for the Mountain," co-written by Jesse Graves and William Wright (*Specter Mountain*, 2018), as well as a nod to Jeff Gundy's poem "Additional Assertions on Soul."

"Father Figures" is dedicated to Dr. John Schultz, Erdal Okumus, Bob Callis, Timmy Bays, Dr. Edwin Benjamin Groner Sr., John Heymann, Martha Heymann, and countless others.

"Three Minutes in Nijmegen" is for the Reintjes family, especially Hans, Ria, Rob, Hanneke.

ACKNOWLEDGMENTS

My gratitude goes out to the editors and readers of the following journals and publications in which many of these poems first appeared, often in earlier versions:

Amethyst Review: "Night Weight"
Appalachian Review: "Northern Mississippi"
The Bookends Review: "A Recollection of Rain"
Braided Way Magazine: "A Sea Strewn Generously"
Broad River Review: "When a Country Is a Metaphor"
Cheat River Review: "Untied"
Delta Poetry Review: "Feed & Seed," "Thirty-Three Football Fields"
Dos Gatos Press: "Texas Hill Country Dusk"
Duality: "The Window"
Expanded Field: "Three Minutes in Nijmegen"
Fourth & Sycamore: "Photograph of My Father in a Tarnished Silver Frame, 1999"
Gnarled Oak: "At the Edge of the Forest," "Mosquitoes"
Gravel: "Alerce Trees," "The Long Light of Late Afternoon," "To the Men Who Laughed at Moses"
Louisiana Literature: "An Evening in Toledo, Ohio"
The Magnolia Review: "The Burn," "Highways Like Frozen Rivers," "Overpopulation," "Sunlight, a Jubilation"
Manzano Mountain Review: "Additional Questions for the Canyon," "Dust Storms May Exist," "Pillars of Light, Hills of White"
Midway Journal: "Footfalls, a Deconstructed Pantoum"
Montana Mouthful: "An Island in the Center of Another World"
New Mexico Review: "Heat Lightning"
One: "Meditation on the Street Art of Valparaíso, Chile," "Orbital"
Opendoor Magazine: "Adonis"
Pine Mountain Sand & Gravel Literary Journal: "Brief Illumination"
Rust & Moth: "Inventory of Pit Stops," "The Window, One Noon"
Shooter Literary Magazine: "State of Being"
The Shore: "C Boarding Group," "If My Physical Ailments Took a Road Trip"

The South Carolina Review: "End of the World"
Speckled Trout Review: "Abandoned Fairytale"
Still: The Journal: "Total Eclipse"
Stirring: "Precarious Cairns"
Sweet Tree Review: "To Which We Are Going"
Third Wednesday: "Corpus Christi, or An Exploration of Time and
    Space," "River Rain"
Whale Road Review: "Conjunctions," "Dead Horses," "A Face in
    the Mirror"
20/20 Vision: Focus on Czech Republic: "Words Spoken with Tenderness"

I'm especially grateful to *Braided Way Magazine* for nominating "A
Sea Strewn Generously" for a Pushcart Prize in 2024, *The Magnolia
Review* for nominating "Highways Like Frozen Rivers" for a Pushcart
Prize in 2018, and those at *Whale Road Review* for nominating "Dead
Horses" for inclusion in the 2019 *Orison Anthology*. I'll also single out
Sandy Coomer for including "Words Spoken with Tenderness" in an
ekphrastic poetry series.

I'm indebted to the wonderful people of Madville Publishing,
especially Linda Parsons, Kim Davis, and Jacqui Davis, for a year of
editorial and design efforts that transformed this manuscript into a
gorgeous physical book. Thank you for seeing merit in these poems
and devoting your energies toward publishing them.

Friend and poet Andrew McFadyen-Ketchum also deserves
special mention for his close reading and editing an early version
of this manuscript. The big changes and microscopic tweaks he
recommended were crucial in wrangling this collection within sight
of its final form.

I'd also like to note other fellow poets who generously took time to
read and offer blurbs for this book: Allison Adair, Destiny O. Birdsong,
Tiana Clark, Jesse Graves, Lily Greenberg, Jeff Gundy, Jeff Hardin,
Elizabeth Hughey, David Meischen, and Joshua Nguyen.

To the teachers from middle school through college who ladled
out kindness, attention, brilliance, and pushed me to think deeply
and create confidently. In particular, Shirley Thornton, Rita Stanley,

Janet McCann. And to the late Larry Heinemann, whose stories and encouragement I continue to take "like sunlight to my heart."

For Sage, my companion of the road. These poems are but a ripple in the river of experiences we shared. I will carry them with me my whole life.

For my mom, who is stronger and more giving than I can fathom. This book exists because of her tender care, her fierce belief. For my twin brother Stephen, who is always with me. For Emily, first reader of many of these poems and the inspiring love of my life, and Eddie, the son I am lucky to parent. And for my dad. I hope to meet him and laugh together in some dimension one distant day, but for now I'll be present in this wondrous world.

Printed in the USA
CPSIA information can be obtained
at www.ICGtesting.com
JSHW020828190824
68375JS00006B/6

9 781956 440850